Original title:
Cracks in the Canopy

Copyright © 2025 Creative Arts Management OÜ
All rights reserved.

Author: Tobias Winslow
ISBN HARDBACK: 978-1-80567-234-0
ISBN PAPERBACK: 978-1-80567-533-4

Veins of Air Through Wood

Whispers of wind make trees sway,
Leaves giggle, they dance and play.
Branches reach like hands at prayer,
Nature's show, a vaudeville affair.

Roots chuckle under muddy ground,
Tickling beetles, oh what a sound!
Each crackle and creak brings delight,
Nature's jokes keep us up at night.

Flickering Sylvan Glimmers

Sunbeams play tag, they dart and dash,
Tickling shadows, they make quite a splash.
Squirrels giggle, they leap and bound,
Each tiny blunder, a sight profound.

Mushrooms peek like old grandmas' hats,
Chortling softly with all the bats.
Light breaks through with a wink so sly,
As laughter echoes, we can't deny.

Broken Patterns Above

The ceiling's a puzzle, bits askew,
Patterns jumbled, a colorful view.
Butterflies ponder their aerial dance,
While birds tumble in a clumsy prance.

Moths play tag in the fading light,
Cackling softly with sheer delight.
The sky's a jester with wild flair,
Giggling clouds float without a care.

Murmurs of a Shattered Sky

Up above, a jigsaw gleams,
Stars break in laughter, shedding dreams.
The moon winks down, a mischievous tease,
As night unfolds its raucous breeze.

While surely tangled, the whole scene sings,
Jokes wrapped in twinkling, cosmic rings.
Now tell me, who wouldn't want to stay,
Under this canopy of goofy play?

Nature's Symphonic Intrusions

Bugs play trumpets, frogs keep time,
Squirrels dance, oh what a rhyme!
The trees sway low with a jolly tune,
While birds chirp notes beneath the moon.

A raccoon winks, wearing a hat,
The butterflies are having a chat.
A caterpillar leads a conga line,
Nature's party, how divine!

The Unearthing of Forgotten Rays

Sunlight peeks through leaves so green,
Finding treasures, oh what a scene!
A cheeky gopher, with shovel in paw,
Digs for laughter, with a smile and a guffaw.

Mice play hide and seek with light,
Chasing shadows in sheer delight.
Each beam a whisper, a tickling tease,
That skips along in a playful breeze.

Leaves that Hold the Sunlight

Leaves chuckle as they catch the rays,
Tickled by sunshine in silly plays.
Their green fingers wave, high with pride,
Only the clouds can dampen their ride.

A leaf hitches a ride on a breezy spree,
Dancing about, as wild as can be.
It swirls and twirls, causing a flurry,
While the tree laughs, "No need to hurry!"

An Overlooked Canvas Above

The sky paints art with splatters of fluff,
Doodles of dragons, but that's not enough.
Clouds wear hats, while raindrops laugh,
Chasing each other, a joyful gaffe.

Paintbrush skies in a whimsical race,
Tickle the sun and give stars a chase.
Nature's whimsy, a light-hearted show,
Above our heads, a masterpiece flow.

The Ethereal Gaps Above

In the forest's quilted sky,
Sunbeams peek, oh my, oh my!
Squirrels dance on leafy beams,
Whispering their nutty dreams.

Birds exchange their gossip light,
About the worms that took to flight.
Fluffy clouds chase tangled vines,
While raccoons spin their silly lines.

Leaves do shuffle, laugh aloud,
As shadows form a goofy crowd.
A dainty breeze joins in the fun,
Tickling branches, everyone done!

Oh the tales the trees could tell,
Of wobbly roots and critters' yell.
Between the bright and broad expanse,
Nature hosts a lively dance.

Beneath the Patchwork Parasol

Underneath the leafy dome,
A spider webs a little home.
Ladybugs wear polka dot,
While bees buzz, "Oh, what a plot!"

Caterpillars munch and chat,
Planning where to nap or spat.
A squirrel shares a snack attack,
While shadows do a silly hack.

Chipmunks gossip, tales unfold,
Of acorn treasures, bright and bold.
The sun sneezes, oh what a mess,
Leaves flutter down in leafy dress.

Beneath this colored tapestry,
Life's a quirky comedy.
Every rustle brings new glee,
Under this great leafy spree.

The Secret Language of Tree Tops

In the boughs where secrets twirl,
Tree frogs croak and squirrels whirl.
Whispers rustle in the air,
Giggling leaves that don't quite care.

Wise old owls throw out their puns,
While chipper birds plot 'Noisy Runs.'
Pine cones giggle, fall with style,
Dropping down in perfect file.

Branches wiggle, having fun,
As sunlight dances, everyone!
A woodpecker's tap, tap, tap,
Mixes up the forest's map.

Up above, the woodlands speak,
A jumbled code, unique and chic.
If you learn their laugh and cheer,
You'll find the forest's heart is clear!

Fleeting Flickers in the Green Vault

Through the branches, lights do flit,
Fireflies play hide and seek a bit.
Upon a leaf, a mouse does prance,
Hitchhiking on a dragonfly's dance.

Glimmers twinkle, fairy play,
As butterflies dip, sway, and splay.
A frog does leap, in joyful cheer,
Splashing in a pond, oh dear, oh dear!

Twilight giggles, crickets sing,
In the cool, they laugh and cling.
A raccoon nods, wearing a grin,
As nighttime whispers softly in.

Hush the world, let the fun ensue,
In the vault where joy shines through.
Each flicker, a giggle, a wink,
Nature sparkles, making us think!

Secrets of the Upper Boughs

Up high where squirrels plot their schemes,
A tree's a stage for their wild dreams.
With acorns tossed like little bombs,
They keep us laughing, oh what qualms!

A crow squawks loud from yonder limb,
Declaring war, his voice quite grim.
Yet all the while, with cheeky glee,
The parrot mocks, 'Come fly with me!'

With branches thick and leaves a-glow,
The secrets hide that birds all know.
A wiggle here, a rustle there,
Turns into laughter, light as air!

So climb up high, take in the scene,
Where every nook has something keen.
In leafy shades, where jokes abound,
Nature's humor knows no bound!

Beneath the Branches

Beneath the limbs where shadows dance,
   A rabbit hops, oh what a prance!
He trips over roots, then shakes his head,
   As if the trees have laughed instead.

The goanna grins from barky cracks,
   While ants salute in tiny packs.
They form a line, a soldier's march,
   All while avoiding a dog's loud arch!

The dappled sun spots every creature,
   Each one a little funny feature.
A cat in stealth, on branch he's found,
   Only to fall—what a silly sound!

So wander here, beneath the green,
   Where every twist is quite the scene.
In laughter soft, let joy be seen,
   Beneath the branches, life's routine!

Luminous Fragments of Nature

In twilight hues, where light is shy,
The fireflies blink like stars on high.
They zip and zoom, a giggly game,
Can you keep up? You'll feel the same!

The raccoon peeks from a knotted nook,
Stealing snacks with a hurried look.
He wears a mask, as if to say,
'It's all in fun, now look away!'

A hedgehog rolls with quite a flair,
Poking fun at all that's rare.
With tiny feet and a wiggly spin,
Who says the forest isn't a win?

So dance with shadows, twirl and laugh,
Take in the moments, a cherished half.
For in this glow, with joy so bright,
Nature's comedy makes spirits light!

Gleaning from the Gaps

In tangled greens, the secrets peek,
Where mischief hides, it's far from meek.
A fox can slip through bushes wide,
With laughter trailing as he slides.

From missing leaves, a chipmunk beams,
He gathers snacks, fulfilling dreams.
Each little peek, each careful try,
Turns ordinary to the most sly!

The breeze whispers through every gap,
As if to share a silly map.
'Take a left at the cantankerous tree,
And find your giggles waiting for thee!'

So venture forth into the cheer,
With every step, find laughter near.
In nature's puzzle, joyous spritz,
What fun it is, this playful blitz!

Drifting Thoughts Amongst the Branches

Squirrels giggle in the tree,
Chasing shadows, wild and free.
Leaves are hats on their heads,
Finding laughter where they tread.

A crow caws jokes, oh so bright,
While chipmunks dance in sheer delight.
Each twig a stage for their play,
In the green sky, they sway away.

Dreams of the Canopy Above

A raccoon dreams in the sun's warm glare,
Of feasts that float in the sweet, cool air.
A picnic up high with a berry tart,
Though fighting squirrels is not for the faint of heart.

Nestled under a leafy shield,
The antics of critters are hilariously revealed.
With acorn hats, they take their stand,
While the wind applauds with a gentle hand.

Whispers Beneath the Leaves

The grasshoppers speak in a buzzing tone,
With tales of mischief held in their drone.
Each rustling leaf has a secret to tell,
Of gossiping frogs who croak very well.

Under the canopy, laughter rings out,
While ants march forth, their pride in no doubt.
A worm in pajamas shares dreams grand,
Of being the king of this leafy land.

Shattered Shadows Above

In the dance of light, the shadows collide,
With a giggle, the sun bugs decide.
A lizard in shades glides by with flair,
While the sunbeams tug and pull at their hair.

High above, a buzz of glee,
As butterflies flutter about like a spree.
In their colorful outfits, they sway with mirth,
Creating a show of joy and worth.

Eclipsed Sunbeams

In the forest where light plays,
Shadow socks hide sunbeams' rays.
Squirrels wear shades, think they're cool,
While owls hoot in their own school.

A chipmunk laughs, a tree stump grins,
As dances begin where daylight thins.
The sun peeks through, then hides again,
While nature's giggle rings through the glen.

On lazy branches, laughter lingers,
With butterflies fluttering like singers.
The breeze joins in this merry show,
While shadows take a bow and go.

Behold this jolly light parade,
Where sunbeams tease, and shade is made.
Underfoot, the laughter's crunch,
Nature's party, let's all munch!

The Inbetween of Willow and Wish

In whispers soft, the willows sway,
A dance of dreams, they laugh and play.
Beneath the bough, a bug does flip,
While mice rehearse their stand-up skit.

The fairies tease, with twinkling lights,
As daisies bloom and spark delight.
Magic's brewed in the air, you see,
While wishers hope as bubbles flee.

A hedgehog dons a tiny hat,
And winks at frogs who chat, just chat.
Whispers swirl like autumn leaves,
For nature's laughter, our hearts believes.

So revel here, where wishes sprout,
In silliness, there's no doubt.
In the space between, we find a boon,
Where sunlight winks like an old cartoon!

Nature's Luminal Embrace

Amid the trees where shadows hide,
Nature takes us on a ride.
A rabbit hops, a grin so wide,
While sunlight sparkles, full of pride.

With giggles bright from blades of grass,
And ladybugs, they dance and pass.
Each ray of light a playful tease,
As fireflies wink with such great ease.

"Mice can't fly!" a crow caws loud,
Yet on a cloud, they'll make him proud.
A turtle sings a funny tune,
While shadows twist beneath the moon.

So join the fun where silliness thrives,
In this embrace, where nature jives.
With blooms of laughter, we're set free,
In nature's light, let's all agree!

The Story Beneath Sky and Leaf

Underneath the leafy shroud,
A secret world laughs out loud.
The sun tickles the dewdrops bright,
While clovers giggle at their sight.

A beatle's band begins to play,
With snails in line to sway away.
The clouds high five, the sun does wink,
As breezes blow and flowers think.

A tale unfolds where shadows meet,
With bunnies bouncing to the beat.
Pretend the sun's a shiny crown,
While nature giggles, never frown.

So come and join this merry plot,
Where every moment hits the spot.
Under sky and leaf, we weave,
Silly stories we believe!

Splinters of Sunlight

A squirrel darts with acorn tight,
He stumbles on a beam so bright.
A dance of rays starts shining down,
While woodpeckers just tease and clown.

The leaves above are all askew,
Sunlight slips through like it has to.
A comical chase of shade and light,
As if the forest is putting on a fight.

Frayed Edges of Green

Beneath the branches, laughter plays,
With butterflies in silly ways.
They flit and float, but then they fall,
While ants march proudly, standing tall.

A vine swings in an awkward bend,
Entangled friends who can't descend.
The wobbly knots on every tree,
Make nature chuckle, wild and free.

Chasms in the Treetops

The birds have formed a cheeky crew,
They gossip and they sing, it's true.
A parrot tells a joke so wild,
While other birds just laugh and smiled.

A gap appears within the leaves,
Where sunlight dances, nature weaves.
The branches wave like hands in glee,
Creating shadows, just look and see!

Echoes in the Grove

The breeze plays tag with whispers sweet,
As raccoons groove on nimble feet.
They trip and tumble, with a flair,
Turning woodland into a fair.

Laughter echoes, the trees remark,
On silly antics in the park.
With every rustle, nature grins,
In this wild world, the fun begins!

Dreams Interwoven in Canopy Gaps

In shadows where the sunlight weaves,
Squirrels dance like they own the leaves.
Beneath a sunbeam's playful nudge,
A butterfly flirts with a gentle smudge.

With hats made of petals, the flowers prance,
Their colors a riot, a wild romance.
Laughter echoes through branches and twine,
As birds start a band with a herbal design.

A woeful frog joins the merry song,
Croaking offbeat, but proud and strong.
Nature's own circus, absurd and divine,
In the gaps above, misfits align.

Light's Sculptural Breach

When sunlight breaks like a comic strip,
Snails grab glasses for a coffee sip.
Mice in tuxedos cheer the display,
While shadows throw a dance-party ballet.

Patches of gold where it shouldn't be,
Casting shadows on a laughing bee.
The woodland painting a clumsy scene,
With every drop making the antics keen.

Under the mischief, roots spread wide,
Worms play poker with fireside pride.
A squirrel whispers secrets of moonlight's plea,
As dance partners trip on a branch with glee.

The Enigma of the Fractured Leaf

A leaf fell down, with a curious wink,
Wondering why the trees never drink.
It twirled through air, like a clueless cat,
Landing on a gopher's stylish hat.

The grass giggled, tickling its side,
"Don't take it hard, just enjoy the ride!"
While dandelions puff, giving gentle cheer,
"Life's a wild ride! Forget your fear!"

In laughter of petals caught in the breeze,
A riddle unfolds 'neath the maple trees.
Who knew such chaos could bring such delight,
As the leaf mumbled jokes in the fading light?

The Haunting Melodies of Light and Dark

Ghosts of dusk play a jumbled tune,
With fireflies flashing like a cartoon.
Whispers of night twist through the pine,
As crickets compose the weirdest line.

Moonbeams prance on a pond's cool skin,
Inviting frogs for a spin and a grin.
Stars tap dance on shadows that sway,
While owls watch closely, critiquing the play.

Nonsense reigns in this vibrant show,
As misfits mingle, each stealing the glow.
Beneath the twinkling, an uproar does spark,
In a gleeful symphony of light and dark.

The Sun's Trajectory Through the Green

The sun gleefully hops, much like a frog,
Bouncing off branches, singing its log.
Dancing with shadows on the forest floor,
It giggles at clouds, yet craves to explore.

Leaves poke their heads like curious kids,
Whispering secrets, sharing their bids.
"Who'll catch the light in this leafy game?"
They wave at the sun and cheer it by name.

A squirrel, all quirky, chews on a nut,
Keen on the sunbeam that tickled his gut.
He leaps up high, to outshine the star,
Then tumbles back down, a comedic avatar.

As beams of sunlight play peek-a-boo,
The tree trunks chuckle, their bark wears the hue.
Nature's a stage, all riddled with jests,
Where laughter and sunlight collide with quests.

Nature's Fragile Harmony

A bird flaps its wings in a wobbly flight,
Crashing through branches, oh what a sight!
The flowers just giggle, their petals a-peel,
At the dancer who fumbles, yet sways with zeal.

Bumblebees buzz with a clumsy refrain,
They trip over pollen, then dance in the rain.
The daisies are chuckling, they nod and they bow,
At these lumpy musicians who sing with a wow.

Tall grasses gossip, they sway with delight,
As breezes tease leaves, they shimmer and fight.
A worm joins the fun, wriggling with ease,
"I'm the king of the soil!" he shouts with a tease.

Together they laugh, in this verdant show,
Nature's own circus, with a hearty glow.
All creatures united, in humor they find,
A fragile harmony that's silly and kind.

Where Light Meets Leaf

Sunlight tiptoes like a cat in the night,
Peeking through leaves, oh what a delight!
It tugs at a twig and shimmies around,
Painting warm patterns on the soft ground.

In this leafy realm, mischief abounds,
Where shadows play tag and no one stands ground.
A chubby raccoon plays hide and seek,
Wearing a mask, oh so cheeky and sleek.

A butterfly flutters, its dance full of glee,
Laughing at branches that sway just to see.
"Catch me if you can!" it flaps with a grin,
While sunlight and laughter spin tales of kin.

As dusk starts to settle, the leaves start to sigh,
The sun waves goodbye, a twinkle in the sky.
Yet tomorrow it promises to shine and to play,
Where light meets the leaf in a joyful display.

The Canopy's Hidden Heart

Deep in the woods, where the laughter gets loud,
The canopy chuckles beneath its green shroud.
A fox trips over roots, lands with a thud,
Covered in leaves, he giggles in mud.

The vines hang low, like a cosmic joke,
Tickling the toes of a wandering bloke.
"Dance with me, nature!" the trees call in tune,
As squirrels join in, beneath the bright moon.

A gnome peeks out from a pocket of shade,
With a wink, he unveils the jokes nature made.
"We're all here for fun, let's not play coy,
In this jumbled heart, nature's pure joy!"

From acorns and ferns to the birds in the air,
All creatures unite in this whimsical affair.
Underneath the canopy's quirky embrace,
Laughter and life find their snug, silly place.

Frayed Edges of the Arboreal

Up in the trees, where squirrels play,
Leaves do a dance, then drift away.
A branch creaks loud, what a surprise!
The bird on it jumps, oh how he flies!

A family of ants threw a picnic spree,
Under a leaf, as grand as can be.
But just as they chewed on crumbs of bread,
A raindrop fell, making quite a spread!

Bark wears a coat of lichen so bright,
Complaining about bugs, oh what a sight!
"Wear bug spray!" they shout, but who would care?
While hiding beneath their leafy lair.

So next time you gaze at trees so tall,
Remember their quirks, embrace them all.
For the giggles of nature, they won't wait,
In the frayed edges, there's much to celebrate!

Lattice of Broken Sunbeams

Sunbeams scattered, a playful game,
The trees jostle gently, who's to blame?
A light-up show, the forest's delight,
While squirrel acrobats take to flight!

Fungi giggle, all round and spry,
Mushrooms hiding, oh me, oh my!
One gave a wink, then let out a cheer,
"Come join my party, it's wild in here!"

The shadows chuckle, with ghostly glee,
"Who's that peeking? Is it you or me?"
The breeze whispers secrets, a soft, silly tune,
Making leaves sway, like a lively cartoon.

So in this forest, where laughter abounds,
Check for surprises that may come around.
With every sunbeam that dances so free,
Life's just a jest, in this leafy spree!

Under the Fractured Shadows

Under the shadows where giggles reside,
The trees have secrets they can't let slide.
A raccoon in sunglasses, striking a pose,
While the owls roll their eyes at his silly clothes.

The breeze cracks jokes, leaves shake with cheer,
As chubby little bunnies hop in near.
"Do I look fluffy?" one asked with a grin,
"To make us laugh, let the fun begin!"

Bug-eyed beetles may start to conspire,
Plotting mischief, their hearts full of fire.
"Let's switch places," one said with a laugh,
"Your green is so pretty, I'll take a giraffe!"

So slip into shadows, let silliness reign,
As whispers and chuckles weave through the grain.
For nature's a playground, so light and bizarre,
Where laughter abounds, life's a bright star!

Sunlight's Daring Dives

Sunlight leaps in, a splash of delight,
Bouncing off leaves, a dazzling sight.
It tiptoes lightly on branches so green,
Tickling the ferns as if they're a scene!

A chipmunk yells, "Catch me if you dare!"
With shadows in tow, they race through the air.
Each twist and turn in the dappled light,
Leaves the squirrels giggling, oh what a sight!

Beneath the bright canopy, laughter does grow,
A conga line forms, with no sign of slow.
The ladybugs join, with tiny red flair,
As sunlight continues its daring affair.

So when you walk beneath limbs up high,
Let the sun's antics lift your spirits and fly.
For every beam's bounce, every jump and dive,
Brings joy to the forest, keeping dreams alive!

The Tree's Silent Sigh

A squirrel plays hide and seek,
With acorns that look rather meek.
The branches groan and sway,
As whispers of laughter stray.

Leaves rustle in a breezy cheer,
And find a new friend in a deer.
They chat about the weather,
While debating who's the better.

The bark's got stories to share,
Like who forgot their underwear.
Yet roots just chuckle at the fuss,
Dirt-stained feet, they do not trust.

The sun's rays dance and prance,
While shadows join the silly dance.
All in a day's playful fun,
In the shade, where joy is spun.

Awakenings in the Forest Floor

Mushrooms peek with silly hats,
Each claims to be the king of spats.
They giggle and tease the ferns,
While the sleepy worm quietly churns.

A robin sings with great delight,
And gives the sleepy leaves a fright.
'Bugs and worms, get up and play!'
No sleeping in, not today!

Underfoot, the soil's alive,
As tiny ants begin to strive.
They form a line for a grand parade,
While the beetles show off their braid.

A sunbeam slips through leafy lanes,
And tickles the toes of passing pains.
Nature's laugh, a joyful roar,
Awakens life forevermore.

Fissures of Nature's Artistry

A painter's brush with hues so bright,
Covers bark with charming blight.
Where colors clash and merge in fun,
A masterpiece by nature's sun.

The flowers joke, 'Let's stand tall!'
While petals waltz, they risk a fall.
'Watch me twirl, I'm bright and bold!'
While laughing leaves just watch untold.

Insects bustle, giggle and glide,
Playing tag from side to side.
Even the fungi join the game,
Mushroom caps take on a name.

Nature's palette, wild and free,
Is filled with quirks and harmony.
Each crack and line tells our tale,
In joyous whispers on the veil.

When Nature's Tapestry Unravels

A spider spins a yarn so grand,
While squirrels lend a helping hand.
They tangle threads of leaf and vine,
In a comical design divine.

A weaver bird sings with flair,
'This nest is best, don't you dare!
My twigs are perfect, smooth and neat,'
While the barbet claims another seat.

Branches sway with a happy tune,
Beneath the sky, a laughing moon.
Nature giggles at each mishap,
Creating joy in every flap.

The wind joins in, a playful guest,
Stirring up the feathered nest.
When nature laughs, all hearts can lift,
As vines and leaves share the funny gift.

The Light that Slips Through

A squirrel named Chuck with a twinkle in eye,
Danced through the branches, his spirit so spry.
He'd leap from the boughs, what a comical sight,
Till he landed in shadows, not quite getting right.

The sunbeams would giggle as they tried to sneak in,
Tickling the grass where the fun would begin.
They'd play peek-a-boo with the leaves overhead,
While Chuck scurried round with his quirky old spread.

The shadows would chuckle, they'd stretch and they'd yawn,
As Chuck chased the light from the dusk until dawn.
But the glimmers would laugh, always managing to flee,
While Chuck, in his antics, just made a mess of tree.

So remember dear friends, when you're under the trees,
A squirrel may be dancing — if you laugh, you might please.
For light can be tricky, like Chuck in his game,
But chasing those rays is what makes it less tame.

Chasing Shadows in the Groves

There once was a cat with a penchant for shade,
Whiskers in waltz, as he skidded and swayed.
He'd pounce on a shadow, all slick and sly,
Only to find it would blush and then fly.

The trees whispered secrets, they rustled with glee,
While Mr. Whiskers, well, he pondered quite free.
"Why do they vanish when I'm close to their reach?
Are shadows elusive? A lesson to teach?"

He'd tumble and roll, chasing wisps of despair,
Tripping on roots like he hadn't a care.
The laughter of leaves would echo through air,
As he plotted and planned for the next daring dare.

In the grove all the critters would shake with delight,
At the sight of a cat on a comical flight.
For what's more absurd than a cat chasing dark,
When the sunshine above holds a whimsical spark?

The Ethereal Gaps in Greenery

In a meadow so bright where the laughter convened,
A rabbit named Lou, he had quite the routine.
He'd hop in the humor of places unknown,
Through spaces of sunlight, he'd frolic and moan.

The daisies would giggle, they stood side by side,
As Lou zoomed through petals with whimsical pride.
He'd zoom through the gaps, playing tag with the breeze,
While the shadows just watched, hoping to tease.

"Where do you think you're going?" the tall grass would jeer,
As Lou leapt and glimmered, motivated by cheer.
With every clumsy twirl, he would tumble and bounce,
While the sunlight then winked, like it had quite the pounce.

"Oh how funny!" the butterflies fluttered in flight,
At the sight of dear Lou, who was chasing the light.
For laughter can sneak through those breaks in the trees,
As joy paints the landscape with each giggling breeze.

A Tapestry of Holes and Hues

In the jungle where shadows play,
A frame of forgetfulness leads the way.
Leafy hats with holes for eyes,
The trees chuckle beneath the skies.

Mismatched patches hold secrets tight,
Where squirrels dance in topsy-turvy flight.
Colors splatter where twigs do bend,
Nature's quilt with threads that blend.

The light stumbles through the jest,
With ghosts of flowers in funny vests.
It giggles as it wiggles through,
A patchwork made for me and you.

In laughter's grip, we weave our tale,
With whims and wonders on the trail.
So come and skip, let worries flee,
In this tapestry, wild and free!

The Shimmer of Revealed Beauty

Sunlight peeks in with a giggle,
Through the leaves, it starts to wriggle.
Little beams in a game of hide,
With winks and twirls, they slide and glide.

A patch of light stirs every leaf,
In a dance of joy—what a belief!
Nature's brush, with colors so bold,
Painting smiles in subtle gold.

Under arches of gorgeously stained,
The silly shadows are unrestrained.
They frolic and hop, a puppet show,
With radiant laughs that softly flow.

Oh, look at the play of gleam and shade,
A twinkling sight that won't ever fade.
In silliness wrapped, beauty shines bright,
As laughter erupts in the warm daylight.

Where the Branches Whisper

In the hush of trees that laugh so sweet,
Branches gossip with a rhythmic beat.
"Did you hear about the silly crow?
He tried to dance but stubbed his toe!"

Leaves gossip like they're on a spree,
Whirling stories in a spiraled glee.
Each breeze a chuckle, every rustle a tease,
As the woods burst forth in joyous ease.

Laughter loops through the tangled vines,
An echo of merry, their spirit shines.
With whispers fluttering, they have their say,
"This tree is older, but I'm more trendy today!"

In this realm of whimsy and cheer,
Nature's jesters are ever near.
So lend an ear, and join the dance,
As the branches twirl in their merry prance.

An Immersion in Nature's Excursion

Step inside, the woods await,
An adventure that's truly first-rate.
With backpacks stuffed with laughter and fun,
A day with nature has just begun.

Frogs in bow ties leap in delight,
Wishing on stars in the warm twilight.
Each flower wiggles, dressed in bright,
As critters chime in with sheer delight.

Through bubbling brooks and grassy green,
A wobbly ant parade can be seen.
They march with pride, no worries unfold,
With little hats that shimmer like gold.

Nature's funny, a jestful spree,
In every nook, a whimsical glee.
So, pack your humor and come on through,
In this vibrant escape, just me and you!

The Gaps that Let the Light Dance

In the jungle, light does sway,
Through openings where shadows play.
A disco ball of sunlit beams,
Nature's punchline, it seems!

The leaves they wiggle, twist, and dive,
As if they're teaching light to jive.
A tango here, a waltz up there,
The forest floor is quite a fair!

With every step, a giggle threads,
Beneath our feet, the laughter spreads.
Who knew that sunlight loved to prance?
Come join the leaves in their strange dance!

So next time you take a stroll,
Look up and join this leafy role.
In this wild, wacky, leafy show,
Where light and laughter freely flow!

Splintered Auras above the Earth

Above the earth, the sunlight beams,
Through splinters, it crafts silly dreams.
A wink of light, a cheeky glare,
The trees all giggle, without a care!

The branches bend like dancers' backs,
While squirrels giggle at the cracks.
They zoom and zip, like little sprites,
In this canopy of punchy lights!

The hues of green and golden rays,
Turn ordinary into a craze.
A kaleidoscope of nature's grin,
Where the wild whimsy can begin.

So come on, laugh, don't be so stern,
Join nature's quirky, raucous turn.
In splintered auras, joy awaits,
In sunny patches, make some mates!

Hues of Hidden Horizons

In hidden heights, the colors play,
With every hue, they joke away.
Emerald jokes and sapphire glee,
Painting the sky, wild and free!

Every shadow has a grin,
While daisies snicker, let's begin!
A vibrant canvas up above,
Covered with laughter, light, and love!

The tussled branches whisper soft,
As if to say, "Let's lift off!"
Beneath the canopy, life spins,
In this circus where fun begins.

So look for smiles in every hue,
Nature's laughter, bright and true.
With hidden colors, join the cheer,
And let your spirit wander here!

Fissures in the Forest Dome

In the forest dome, where shadows peek,
Little voices softly speak.
"Hey, over here!" the sunlight calls,
Through fissures wide, the humor sprawls!

With every crack, a grin appears,
As foliage giggles with no fears.
A tickle from the breezy air,
Transforms the woods into a fair!

The light leaps high, then tumbles down,
The trees, they laugh; they wear a crown.
In this green world, hilarity's bold,
Where stories of sunlight are told.

So find a seat beneath the beams,
Where nature shares its silly dreams.
In the dome of greens, we all belong,
Where laughter rings, and life is strong!

When Light Pricks the Silence

In the woods where shadows play,
Sunbeams giggle, dance away.
A squirrel sneezes, and oh dear,
The echoes ripple far and near.

Mossy carpet, vibrant green,
Spots of sun can be quite mean.
They peek through leaves, the little spies,
While tree trunks hold their secret sighs.

A bird drops snacks in careless glee,
As if to tease, 'Come play with me!'
But in this light, one can't ignore,
The laughter that we can explore.

So hark! An acorn's quiet plop,
A nature's jest that makes you stop.
For when the sun wants to be bright,
It tickles silence, oh what a sight!

The Estranged Geometry of Trees

In a forest, roots in flight,
Branches twist in pure delight.
Angles sharp, but oh so grand,
Nature's math we can't quite understand.

Leaves like hats on every head,
Wobble gently, it's all well-fed.
They whisper jokes in the cool breeze,
While trunks stand tall, just trying to please.

Some trees arch back, like they don't care,
While others pose with a dapper flair.
A knotty laugh, a knobby rib,
In this odd world, we dance and jig.

So grab your compass, lose your way,
In angles keen, we'll laugh and play.
For every branch is a wild spree,
A funny dance of geometry!

Patterns Above the Periphery

Look up high, a splendid view,
Where leaves form signs, both bold and blue.
Latticework of laughter tumbles down,
Nature's quilt, a leafy crown.

Clouds poke fun, they race and tease,
While sunbeams slip through with ease.
The flora giggles at the sun's chase,
As shadows shimmy in a playful embrace.

A spider spins a web of jokes,
Above the heads of chatting folks.
They giggle as they catch the light,
In the silly maze, oh what a sight!

Each rustling leaf joins the jest,
Nature's laughter at its best.
So gaze above with glee and cheer,
For patterns hum as day draws near!

An Expose of Nature's Silk

In the glade, a soft unveil,
Nature's threads tell the tale.
Silken trails drape low and wide,
A magician's cloak where secrets hide.

Worms wear bows and spiders glide,
While bees in tuxes proudly stride.
In this assembly, what a ruckus,
Fashioned splendidly, oh so circus!

A butterfly drums with wings so bright,
Throwing disco parties in the light.
And ladybugs in polka dots,
Dance around in merry knots.

Oh, nature's friends, such crafty tricks,
They spin and twirl with nimble kicks.
For silk is spun with laughter's thread,
In this grand ball, we're all well fed!

Whispers Through the Gaps

In the forest, secrets spill,
Squirrels gossip, what a thrill!
Birds swap tales, a light banter,
While old trees chuckle and slanter.

Mushrooms giggle, hiding shy,
As ants march by with a tiny sigh.
Rabbits trade their silly dreams,
Beneath the sun's warm, poking beams.

The wind plays tricks, a sudden sway,
Leaves dance around in a playful way.
Even shadows start to tease,
Playing hopscotch with the breeze.

Nature's jest, a joyful spree,
With laughter blending, wild and free.
Beneath the green, the fun can flow,
In tiny spaces where wonders grow.

Shadows Beneath the Leaves

Beneath the green, where oddities roam,
Little critters call this home.
A raccoon jokes with a sleepy owl,
While beetles spin tales with a scowl.

Breeze whispers silly lines of cheer,
As mossy carpets tickle near.
Saplings giggle in soft light,
Joking 'bout starlight, oh what a sight!

A worm's got moves, a wiggly dance,
In muddy puddles, they take a chance.
Each laugh echoes through twisted vines,
Sharing the joy in nature's signs.

Shadows below, a playful sight,
Beneath the leaves, there's pure delight.
In every nook where laughter strives,
The forest thrives with goofy lives.

Fractured Light at Dusk

Flickering suns through branches play,
As fireflies join the evening sway.
Lightning bugs, in suits of glow,
Practice their waltz, stealing the show.

Twilight giggles, tints in hues,
Of orange, pink, with a hint of blues.
The moon rolls in with a cheeky grin,
While shadows ponder where to begin.

Stars drop puns on the roof of night,
Raccoons toss orbs in a playful flight.
Crickets hum a jazzy tune,
As sleepy heads nod to the silver moon.

Fractured beams of day's soft end,
In the dark, even shadows blend.
Nature's jesters fill the dusk,
With laughter sweet like the smell of musk.

Shadows of an Overgrown Sky

Above the trees, the clouds parade,
Like fluffy creatures, unafraid.
A sunbeam trips over branches wide,
Sending shadows on a joyride.

Dandelions toss their wicked hair,
As butterflies flirt without a care.
Carpenter bees drill with finesse,
Building homes in their wild mess.

The sky is painted with silly schemes,
As daydreams burst, or so it seems.
Giggling lizards bask in the sun,
Where all things green just want to run.

In overgrown fields, antics await,
With whimsical creatures, oh so great.
Nature's jest fills the broad expanse,
In shadows of laughter, everyone loves to dance.

Fractured Light Beneath the Boughs

The sun peeked through, a playful tease,
A dance of shadows beneath the trees.
The squirrels plotting, a heist so grand,
Stealing the shine to bury in sand.

A bird so bold takes a sunny spot,
Singing a tune that's hot on the trot.
While ants wear shades in their tiny parade,
Strutting on paths they've confidently made.

Each beam, a wink, a giddy delight,
As laughter echoes through the soft light.
Nature's humor, a show on display,
With giggles and grins, it's a bright ballet.

So let's raise a toast to this jolly show,
Where every odd angle steals the glow.
In a world where the sunshine loves to play,
Fun's the best rule — come join the fray!

Secrets of the Timbered Sky

Eyes to the treetops, secrets galore,
A riddle of leaves that dance and soar.
The creatures up high whisper their fables,
A drama unfolds—no scripts, just labels.

The sun's in on it, a gossiping friend,
While shadows suggest a wild weekend.
Owls hold court, with their wisecrack ways,
As the moon just chuckles at their sunlit plays.

Deep in the boughs, a lemon tree grows,
Where citrusy jokes sprout like petals and prose.
The chatter is ripe, nature's punchlines fly,
Cracking up chirps that burst from the sky.

So join the party, it's never too late,
Under the laughter, the woodland's great state.
The timbered sky holds a giggle or two,
With humor above and below, fresh as dew!

Splintered Veils of Green

Through curtains of green, the chuckles emerge,
A tangle of vines with a whimsical urge.
Where rabbits, with flair, juggle bouncy bright blooms,
And snicker at foxes in clumsy costumes.

A breeze plays tricks, with a wink and a roll,
Turning the ferns into green-fuzzed moles.
Caterpillars strut as they flaunt their new moves,
In this leafy ballet, every bug grooves.

With sunbeams as props, they steal every pose,
While mice in white gloves master ballet toes.
Here, wild things giggle, with mischief and cheer,
A carnival treasure, we're glad to be here.

So let's soak it in, this nature's delight,
With splintered veils swirling, a colorful sight.
In the theater of green, our laughter will glean,
The fun in the wild, and the joy in between!

Radiance Through the Rift

A gap in the leaves reveals a bright show,
Casting quirky shadows that giggle and grow.
Dance floors of twilight where fireflies wink,
While night creatures gather to share and to think.

With sprites making mischief in dribbles of light,
They juggle the stars through the soft veil of night.
Each flicker a story, each glow a delight,
As laughter unfurls on this magical flight.

The breeze hums a tune, an airy soft score,
With echoes of fun blending more and more.
A raccoon in a hat gives the crowd quite a show,
With tales of the moon and how deep it can go.

So we'll linger beneath, where the whimsy takes root,
In the caverns of laughter where mischief's a hoot.
Through rifts, there's a glimmer, of joy shining bright,
In the glow of the night, everything feels just right!

Dappled Echoes in the Wilderness

In a forest so bright, a squirrel did prance,
He tripped on a branch, lost his daring stance.
With acorns a-flying, he launched through the air,
The trees shook with laughter, a comical flare.

A rabbit nearby wore a crown made of leaves,
As he hosted a party, oh, what a tease!
The owls rolled their eyes at the dance of the fawn,
And a raccoon in the corner was snoring till dawn.

Sunlight peeked through like a spotlight of cheer,
Illuminating antics that only we hear.
As critters performed on the woodland's grand stage,
With nature as witness, they all turned the page.

So here in the wild, where the whimsy takes flight,
The laughter of creatures fills day and night.
Each rustle and giggle tells tales of delight,
Beneath the bright canopy, everything's right.

When the Sky Meets the Soil

There's a debate going on, 'twixt the clouds and the ground,
Who's more important? A question profound!
The soil grumbles softly, 'Without me, you're naught,'
The sky giggles back, 'But I give you thought!'

Down by the brook where the shadows do play,
A fish wore a hat that was quite out of sway.
The frogs formed a band with their lily-pad drums,
Joining in chorus, the whole river hums.

One day a raindrop decided to camp,
He landed on soil, said, 'Time for a stamp!'
But the ground held its breath, 'You can't stay for long!'
The raindrop just laughed, 'I'll bounce back—what's wrong?'

So the sky and the soil shared jokes without end,
In a climate of humor, they blossomed as friends.
With laughter abounding where earth meets the sky,
Nature's own comedy, oh my, oh my!

Untold Stories Among the Foliage

In a tangle of vines with a twist and a turn,
A mischievous mouse had a secret to learn.
With whispers of tales carried through the breeze,
He gathered the bugs for a moment of tease.

They spoke of a crow with a voice like a bell,
Who dreamed of being a comedian—oh, what a sell!
He practiced his jokes with a squawk and a flap,
But laughter erupted, sending him in a flap!

When daylight retreats, the shadows grow long,
The whispers of foliage weave together a song.
A caterpillar yawned, 'This show's been grand fun!'
But he fell fast asleep, missing the final pun.

Yet the laughter endured under starlight so bright,
With creatures cocooned in their dreams of delight.
For every leaf rustle and flicker of light,
Told stories amusing, hidden from sight.

The Light's Fragile Pathway

A beam of light juggled through branches and leaves,
It tripped on a shadow and went, 'Goodness, please!'
The sun laughed so heartily, sending rays to assist,
While a nearby breeze chirped, 'You must be persist!'

Dancing through dew like a giggling sprite,
The light twirled and twisted, in sheer pure delight.
But unseen by the world, a moth tried to cheat,
And stumbled ungracefully right under its feet!

The pathway grew wider, with laughter a-pour,
As colors ignited like never before.
Each flicker and shimmer brought smiles to the day,
With sunlight proclaiming, 'Just come out and play!'

So remember this tale of the light on its way,
That joy can be found in the smallest display.
In nature's grand dance, let your laughter ignite,
In the fragile of moments, find joy in the light.

Gaps in Nature's Tapestry

Amid the leaves, a squirrel peeks,
With tiny nuts and funny squeaks.
The sun beams down through patches wide,
Where shadows dance, and birds collide.

A rabbit hops in a sunlit spot,
Wondering why he feels so hot.
The trees above do a little jig,
As branches sway, they dance a gig.

Bees buzz by with a silly hum,
Chasing their friends who feel so glum.
With every turn, they lose the race,
And in a flower, they find their place.

Nature's weave is bright and bold,
With laughter wrapped in greens and golds.
So take a break, enjoy the hee,
In nature's patchwork, wild and free.

Echoes of the Unseen Sun

The hidden star above, so grand,
Whispers secrets to the land.
A duck quacks loud, a comical tone,
In shadows deep, he's not alone.

The shadows stretch, they bend and sway,
As critters frolic, come out and play.
A wise old owl gives a cheeky wink,
His thoughts, it seems, we cannot think.

A chipmunk's dance, on a log so wide,
His tiny heart full of woodland pride.
The sunlight sneaks through tangled vines,
To watch the world in funny designs.

The sun's shy glimmers make us grin,
As laughter echoes where we begin.
So chase the rays, let joy abound,
In nature's theater, where fun is found.

Breaches in the Woodland Roof

In the forest, where mischief stirs,
The raccoons giggle and spin in furs.
One lost a hat in a windy gale,
Now he's a chef with a comical tale.

Mushrooms pop up, like heads of glee,
Waving hello to the buzzing bee.
The ants march on, a silly parade,
Their tiny tune, a funny charade.

Branches arch and twist like clowns,
Hiding secrets in leafy gowns.
A fox in the thicket, a jester sly,
Winks at the world with a knowing eye.

With every crack, laughter blooms,
Beyond the trees, joy surely looms.
Nature's comedy, wild and bright,
A playful scene, pure delight.

Celestial Patches of Disclosure

Stars peek through with a twinkling grin,
As night unfolds and dreams begin.
The moon chuckles at the owl's hoot,
While fireflies dance in their glowing suit.

With every glow, a giggle spills,
As shadows play by the hopeful hills.
A hedgehog spins in a ticklish way,
While crickets sing the night's ballet.

The breeze whispers jokes to the tall grass,
While whispers float like a breezy pass.
Nature laughs in a cosmic show,
And under the stars, we join the flow.

So gaze above at the playful bright,
And let your heart feel the pure delight.
For in these patches, laughter is found,
In every twinkle, joy abounds.

The Luminescent Hunt

In the forest bright, with lanterns in hand,
We searched for the glow with a whimsical band.
A squirrel in a hat danced under the trees,
While mushrooms wore socks in a playful breeze.

The fireflies giggled, flashing their light,
Matching our steps in the warm summer night.
With twinkling sparks soaring, the laughter would rise,
Creating a scene that was filled with surprise.

We spotted a fox with a lantern so grand,
He winked and he whirled, like he'd just made a stand.
His tail swished with glee, lighting up all around,
As we joined in the frolic on soft, leafy ground.

With giggles and grins, we'd capture the glow,
In a dance with the shadows, both friendly and slow.
Our treasure was laughter, like gold in the night,
In a world full of wonders that felt just so right.

Skylit Patches of Wonder

Under a canopy where mischief lives,
We found little spots where the sunshine gives.
A rabbit in bowtie began to compete,
As he bounced through the beams on his nimble feet.

Bright-colored flowers began to applaud,
With petals all waving, it seemed quite odd.
A snail in a top hat offered a wink,
While the breeze played a tune, making us think.

With patches of light like a silly surprise,
We spotted a crow who was wearing some ties.
He'd caw at the branches, with style and with flair,
Chasing after shadows with plumes in the air.

In laughter we tumbled on the soft, mossy bed,
Sharing stories of gnomes and the tricks that they spread.
Under rays so bright, we danced and we spun,
In the joy of the forest, we laughed and we won.

The Interstices of the Living Canopy

Between the green leaves where giggles abound,
We found little gaps where the fun could be found.
A squirrel in sunglasses, so cool and so bold,
Declared he was king of the stories retold.

The sunlight peeped in, creating odd shapes,
While flowers formed teams of comical drapes.
A dance-off commenced in a sunbeam's embrace,
As mushrooms all wobbled in a silly race.

The laughter echoed, bouncing off bark,
As chipmunks donned capes, making their mark.
With a gleeful parade, they strutted with cheer,
And even the trees could not help but appear.

We made merry memories in quirky spots fair,
While creatures all sang out, unaware of our care.
In the merry mischief, we found our delight,
As the forest rejoiced in the whimsical light.

Shades of Light on the Forest Floor

In the dappled glow where the shadows do play,
A frog with a crown proclaimed, "Hip-hop hooray!"
He jumped on a lily, so boldly he leaped,
Scaring poor insects that laughed as they weeped.

Beneath the tall trees where sunbeams did peek,
The ants staged a march for a silly critique.
All donned tiny hats with confetti to spare,
Creating a ruckus, oh what a fanfare!

Raccoons in pajamas were searching for snacks,
While all of the critters just sat on their backs.
A twinkling of fireflies danced in pursuit,
Like stars in the grass that had fallen, how cute!

As giggles and whispers filled woodlands so bright,
We reveled in the charm of this silly sight.
With shapes in the shadows, and dreams made of mirth,
We cherished the magic upon this grand earth.

www.ingramcontent.com/pod-product-compliance
Lightning Source LLC
Chambersburg PA
CBHW071820160426
43209CB00003B/145